Contents

HINDUISM

WORSHIP

FESTIVALS

HISTORY

PEOPLE

MAP: where the main religions began

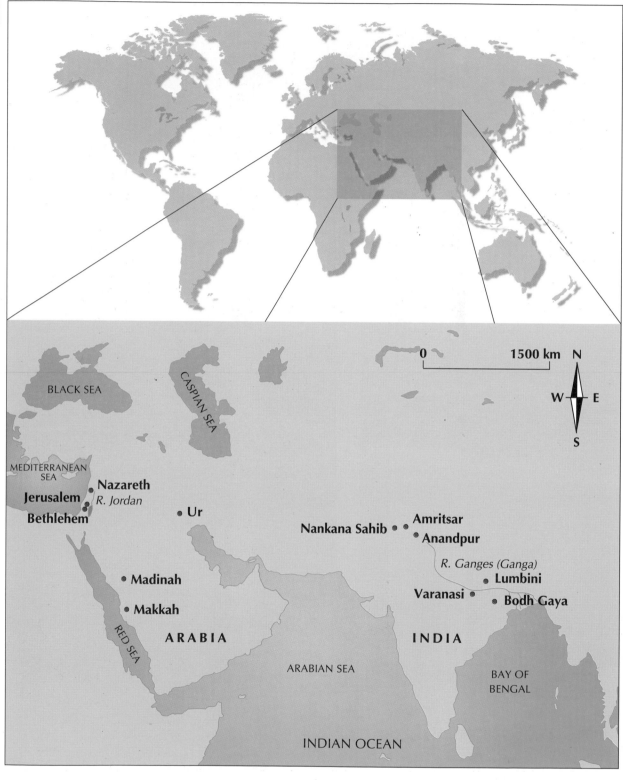

TIMECHART: when the main religions began

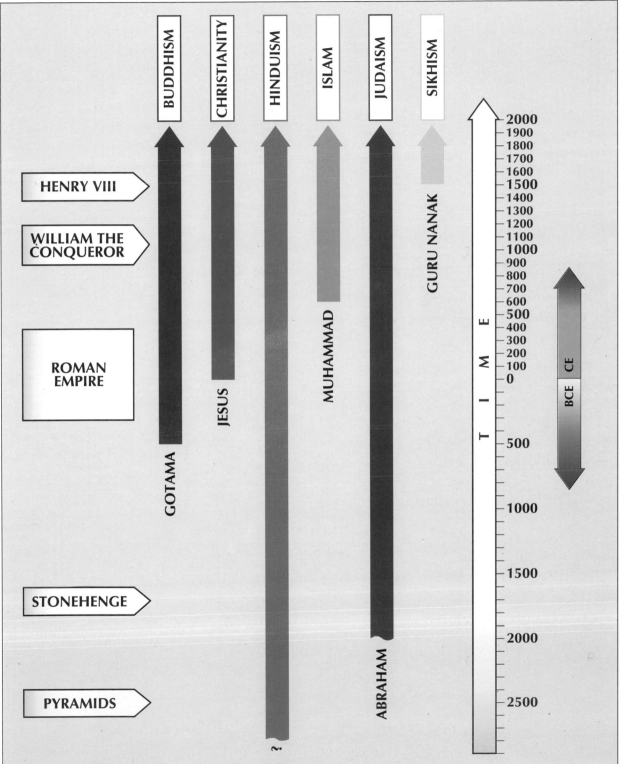

BUDDHISM

CHRISTIANITY

HINDUISM

ISLAM

JUDAISM

SIKHISM

HENRY VIII

WILLIAM THE CONQUEROR

ROMAN EMPIRE

GURU NANAK

GOTAMA

JESUS

MUHAMMAD

ABRAHAM

STONEHENGE

PYRAMIDS

T I M E

2000
1900
1800
1700
1600
1500
1400
1300
1200
1100
1000
900
800
700
600
500
400
300
200
100
0

500

1000

1500

2000

2500

BCE CE

BCE CE

Note about dating systems

In this book dates are not called BC and AD which is the Christian dating system. The letters BCE and CE are used instead. BCE stands for 'Before the Common Era' and CE stands for 'Common Era'. BCE and CE can be used by people of all religions, Christians too. The year numbers are not changed.

Introducing Hinduism

This section tells you something about who Hindus are.

Hinduism is the oldest of the major world religions. It began so long ago that no one really knows how old it is, but it goes back at least 5000 years. The name 'Hindu' comes from an old name for people who lived in part of northern India. Today, over 800 million people living in India are Hindus, and as many again live in other parts of the world.

Hinduism was not begun by any one person, and it developed gradually over more than a thousand years. This means that today it has many different 'branches' and its followers have a very wide range of beliefs and ways of worshipping. Hinduism is a way of life as much as a religion, and different Hindus may believe quite different things without being 'right' or 'wrong'. This book concentrates on things which almost all Hindus would agree with.

What do Hindus believe?

Hindus do not usually talk of their religion as 'Hinduism'. They prefer to call it **Sanatan dharma**. This means 'eternal truths' – in other words, basic teachings which have always been true and always will be. These truths are written about in the Hindu holy books called the **Vedas**. Some of the books contain hymns to be used in worship, others are discussions about important issues. Most Hindus believe that following the teachings of these books is the most important part of their faith.

Hinduism teaches that there is one Great Power. Most Hindus say that this is not a person, and not 'he' or 'she' but 'it'. It is called **Brahman**. Many Hindus would say Brahman can be translated as 'God'. It is everywhere, and everything that exists lives in Brahman all the time. Nothing would exist if God was not in it. Hindus often explain this by using an example. They say that it is like salt dissolved in water. The salt is present even in the tiniest drop of the water, and makes it what it is. In the same way, God is in everything in the universe, and this makes everything what it is. Many Hindus say that this power can be seen most easily through gods. The three main gods are Shiva, Vishnu and Brahma.

Hindu children in London worshipping at home

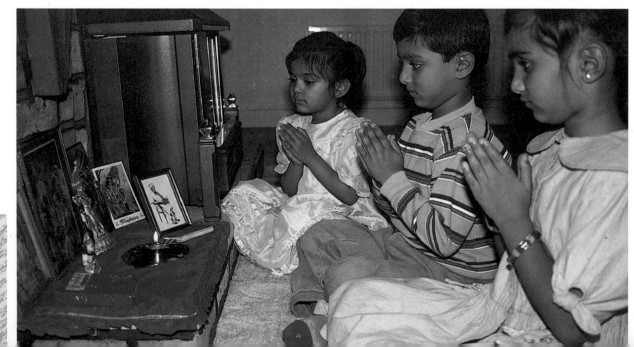

Reincarnation

Another important part of Hindu belief is the idea of **reincarnation**. This is the belief that when you die, your **soul** goes on to live in another person, animal or other being. Where it goes depends on how you have lived in this life. The aim of every Hindu is to become good enough to break out of this cycle of birth and death, so that their soul can become part of Brahman. This will be perfect happiness.

Symbols of Hinduism

The **symbol** often used for Hinduism is made up of **Sanskrit** letters. (Sanskrit is a very old language, in which the Hindu holy books were first composed.) The letters spell the word '**Aum**'. This is said as if it were spelt Ah-oo-m. For Hindus, this sound is **sacred**. It is a way of describing Brahman. Hindu prayers begin with this sound.

The Hindu symbol 'Aum'

New words

Aum sacred Hindu word
Brahman the Great Power
Eternal lasting for ever
Reincarnation belief that a soul is reborn
Sacred very holy
Sanatan dharma 'eternal truth'
Sanskrit old language
Soul a person's spirit
Symbol something which stands for something else
Vedas Hindu holy books

Test yourself

What are the Vedas?

What's Brahman?

What's reincarnation?

Things to do

1 Explain why there are many different branches of Hinduism.

2 What do Hindus believe about Brahman?

3 What is reincarnation? List three things which you think would be good and three things which you think would be bad about being reincarnated.

4 Hinduism is the main religion of India. Find out more about India. Where is it? What's its capital? How many people live there? Write an article explaining what you have found out. (Geography books and encyclopaedias will help.)

Gods and goddesses 1

This section tells you about the most important Hindu gods.

There are thousands of gods and goddesses in Hinduism. When the religion began, the people probably believed that these gods and goddesses really existed. Some Hindus may still believe this, but today most Hindus agree that the gods are not real beings. They are seen as symbols for describing Brahman, the Great Power. Brahman is beyond the understanding of human beings, so the gods and goddesses are ways of showing something which cannot be described. Hindus believe that if they worship Brahman through a god or goddess they can understand, they will find it easier to worship properly.

Trimurti

There are three gods which Hindus believe are the most important. They are Brahma the **creator**, Vishnu the **preserver** and Shiva the destroyer. These three gods are known as the **Trimurti**. They work together in a never-ending pattern. Everything is made, lasts for a time and is then destroyed. This section concentrates on Vishnu and Shiva, because today they are worshipped much more than Brahma.

Vishnu

Vishnu is worshipped under several different names. This is because of his different appearances. Hindus believe that when there is a time of danger for the earth, Vishnu comes to protect it. They believe he has come to earth in nine different bodies, some animal, some human. Two of these appearances are much more important than the others. One was when he came as the god Rama, the other was when he came as the god Krishna.

Rama's story is told in the poem called the Ramayana (see page 15), which is part of the Hindu holy books. He was a prince whose wife was captured by an evil demon. The story includes many adventures before in the end good wins over evil. Krishna is the hero of the Bhagavad Gita, part of a poem called the Mahabharata (see page 14). He is very important, and is worshipped by more Hindus than any other god.

Shiva

Shiva is worshipped by about a quarter of all Hindus. He is the god who destroys, so he controls life and death. Although he can be

An old statue showing Vishnu with Brahma and Shiva

Shiva the Lord of the Dance

frightening, he is also thought of as being kind and easy to please. Shiva destroys things which are old or no longer needed, but this allows new things to happen. He has at least four hands to show that he holds life and death and good and evil. He is often shown as the 'Lord of the dance', and his dance is the energy which keeps the universe moving. Sometimes he is shown dancing on a monster, which he is destroying. The monster is ignorance.

Many Hindu gods and goddesses have several different names, which show different parts of their character. This can be quite confusing, even for Hindus. The important thing to remember is that all the gods and goddesses are ways of describing Brahman the Great Power.

New words

Creator one who makes things
Preserver one who keeps things from decay
Trimurti 'the three gods' – Brahma, Vishnu and Shiva

Test yourself

What's a creator?

What's the Trimurti?

Why does Shiva have four hands?

Things to do

1 Why is the Trimurti so important? Explain how the three gods work together.

2 Explain why Hindus say that the different gods are ways of describing Brahman.

3 Why do you think that Vishnu has come to earth in different forms?

4 Using the text and the picture on this page to help you, draw your own picture of Shiva dancing on ignorance.

Gods and goddesses II

This section tells you about some of the Hindu gods and goddesses who are worshipped most often.

A Hindu can choose to worship any of the thousands of gods or goddesses, or more than one. Their choice often depends on which gods their family worship, or perhaps on an event where they believe one particular god has helped them. Some gods and goddesses are particularly popular.

Shakti

Many of the gods have 'families', and one of the most popular goddesses is Shiva's wife. Like many Hindu gods and goddesses, she has more than one name to show different parts of her personality. She is sometimes called Shakti, the Mother Goddess. In other forms she is called Durga or Kali or Parvati. As Durga, she destroys demons. As Kali, she is often pictured wearing a necklace of skulls, with six or eight hands holding weapons. She is often shown dancing with Shiva. Although she is very frightening, Kali is seen as giving peace to her followers, because she helps them to overcome their fears. As Parvati, however, she is peace-loving and gentle.

Lakshmi

Lakshmi is the wife of Vishnu. She is the goddess of beauty and wealth, and of good fortune. She is not as important as Durga, but many Hindus pray to her especially at New

Kali

Year, asking that the financial year to come will be a good one for them.

Ganesha

Ganesha is the god of wisdom and strength. In the 'god-family', Ganesha is Shiva's son. The stories say that Shiva cut off Ganesha's head by mistake when he was in a temper. He gave Ganesha an elephant's head in its place. This is why Ganesha is always shown with an elephant's head.

Hanuman

Hanuman is the monkey god. He stands for intelligence. In the story of the Ramayana (see page 15), Hanuman helped the prince Rama when his wife Sita had been kidnapped.

The large numbers of gods and the different ways of worshipping mean that Hinduism is a very tolerant religion. Hindus do not claim that the god they worship is the 'right' one – many of the holy books talk of worshipping more than one god. They also do not try to persuade other people to become Hindus. They believe that the most important thing is that each person should worship God in the way that he or she feels to be right for them.

Ganesha

Test yourself

What are Shakti's other names?

What does Ganesha look like?

Who is the monkey god?

Things to do

1 What sort of reasons might a Hindu have for choosing which god to worship?

2 Why do you think Kali is one of the most popular goddesses?

3 What do Hindus say about the way other people worship? What do you think about this?

4 Choose one of the gods or goddesses mentioned in this section. Draw your own picture to show what they look like.

Holy books I

This section tells you about the most important Hindu holy books.

Hinduism has developed over thousands of years. Many different books have been written in that time, praising the gods, describing the correct ways of worship and discussing Hindu beliefs. Most of the holy books are written in Sanskrit, which is one of the oldest languages in the world. Today it is only used for religious purposes. Some of these books are not often read today, but others are still very important.

The Vedas

The Vedas are the oldest of the Hindu holy books. Hindus believe that the Vedas came from God, and they contain basic truths which never change. They go back to about 1200BCE, but they were not collected together and written down for about 3000 years. The teachings were passed down by word of mouth. A father would teach his son the words, the son taught his son, and so on. People in those days were used to remembering things, because very few people could read or write.

The most important Veda is the first. It is called the **Rig Veda**, and contains over 1000 hymns. They are made up of verses called **mantras**. The hymns are really poems praising the 33 gods who control the forces of nature. The other Vedas contain instructions to the priests about how worship should be carried out, and descriptions of religious ceremonies.

The Upanishads

The Upanishads are the last part of each Veda. The name comes from words which mean 'sit down near', and this is how the teachings began. People who wanted to learn from wise men would sit down around them, listening to what they were saying and learning from it. The Upanishads contain discussions about the most important things which Hindus believe, for example, what God is like, and how human beings can know God.

The Laws of Manu

The Laws of Manu are some of the most important law books for Hindus. No one really knows when Manu lived, but he was a wise

Sanskrit (a page from an illustrated copy of the Madhandoya Purana)

teacher whose words were written down by 300CE. There are 2685 verses in the books of the Laws of Manu. They contain instructions about how Hindus should live their lives and show how important it is to follow the teachings of Hinduism in everyday life. They include the punishments for certain crimes, and rules which priests should follow. Many Hindus try to obey all the Laws of Manu.

The Puranas

The Puranas were written down over a period of about a thousand years, after about 500CE. The word 'puranas' means 'olden times'. They are part of the group of holy books which help to explain the Vedas. They contain many well-known stories, and deal mainly with the worship of Brahma, Vishnu, Shiva and Shakti. Altogether there are over half a million verses in the Puranas.

New words

Mantra short sacred text or prayer
Rig Veda first and most important of the Vedas

Test yourself

What are the Vedas?

What are mantras?

What does 'purana' mean?

Things to do

1 Explain how the Vedas were remembered before they were written down. What are the advantages and disadvantages of this method of remembering things?

2 What does 'Upanishad' mean? How did the Upanishads begin?

3 The Laws of Manu are very old. Why do you think Hindus try to obey all of them in their lives?

4 Draw a picture or cartoon-strip which would help you to tell a story to someone who cannot read or write. You could choose a well-known story, or something that has happened to you.

Reading the holy books is an important part of Hindu worship

Holy books II

This section tells you about two important Hindu poems.

There are two long poems which form part of the Hindu holy books. One is called the Mahabharata, the other is called the Ramayana. They are important not just because they are good stories, but also because of the lessons they teach about the religion.

The Mahabharata

The Mahabharata is the longest poem in the world. It has 100,000 verses! It was not written by one person, but was added to by many people over several hundred years. The poem is complicated, because as well as the main story it has many other stories which are included to teach important lessons. The main story is about two royal families. They are cousins, and quarrel over who should be the rightful ruler of the country. One family tricks the other, and war begins. There is a great battle. Before the battle begins, one of the royal princes, Arjuna, talks to the person who is driving his chariot. This person turns out to be the god Krishna in disguise. This is the most famous part of the poem, and it includes the Bhagavad Gita, which is probably the best-loved part of all the Hindu Scriptures.

'Bhagavad Gita' means 'song of the Lord'. Arjuna tells Krishna that he does not want to fight, because the battle is against his cousins, and he does not want to kill his relations. Krishna teaches the prince about his duty and about the right ways for people to worship. The Bhagavad Gita is the most important part of the Scriptures for many Hindus.

This painting shows Krishna and Arjuna before the battle

Dancing the Ramayana (Rama faces Ravana, Hanuman is on the right)

The Ramayana

The Ramayana has 24,000 verses. It is thought to be the work of a man called Valmiki, and was probably written down in about 100CE. It tells the story of Prince Rama and his wife Sita. Prince Rama was an appearance of the god Vishnu. In the story, Rama's father has promised his youngest wife two wishes. She asks for her own son to be made king instead of Rama, and for Rama to be sent away for fourteen years. The king is heartbroken, but has to keep his promise. Rama obeys his father, and with his wife and his brother goes to live in a far-off country. While they are there, Rama's wife Sita is kidnapped by the wicked demon Ravana, who keeps her prisoner on an island. The monkey-god Hanuman helps Rama to find Sita, and Hanuman's monkey army help Rama to win a fierce battle against Ravana. In the battle, Rama kills Ravana, and he and Sita are able to return home. Rama is crowned king, and everything ends happily. Good wins over evil.

The stories in the Mahabharata and the Ramayana can be understood on many different levels. For children, they are exciting stories. For adults, they teach important lessons about the gods and the way to worship. Many Hindu actors and dancers use parts of the stories in their performances.

Test yourself

What's the Mahabharata?

What's the Ramayana?

What does 'Bhagavad Gita' mean?

Things to do

1 Explain why adults and children can all enjoy stories like the Mahabharata and the Ramayana.

2 How many reasons can you think of why the Bhagavad Gita is so important for Hindus?

3 Write a short story of your own in which good wins over evil.

4 Working in small groups, use the information here and any other information you can find, to retell the story of either the Ramayana or the Mahabharata. Illustrate it with drawings.

Worship I

This section tells you about how Hindus worship at home.

Hindus believe that their religion affects everything they do, so everything in their life is worship. Particular forms of worship may include repeating the names of God, listening to or reading the holy books or making offerings. The most common form of worship is called **puja**. This can take place at home or in the temple.

Puja

Puja can happen in many different ways – it may be very simple or very complicated. The rules for making puja are laid down in the Hindu holy books. It involves making offerings to an image or picture of one of the gods or goddesses. An image is called a **murti**, which means 'form'. A murti is intended to help people worship, because it is a way of showing one of the qualities of Brahman.

A Hindu house always has a **shrine** where the murti or pictures are kept. A shrine is a special holy place. Sometimes it may be very simple, just a shelf on the wall. Other shrines may be beautifully decorated. If the house is large enough, the shrine will be in a separate room. If not, it is usually in the kitchen or the mother's bedroom. The murti is surrounded by flowers and perfume, and sometimes pictures of other gods or important Hindus are kept in the shrine as well. There may also be a container of water taken from the River Ganga (often called the Ganges), which Hindus believe is a sacred river.

Worship at home takes place at least once a day. The point of the worship is to spend time in the presence of God, so Hindus prepare for it and perform it very carefully. If there is a murti in the shrine, it is washed, dried and touched with special coloured powders. It may have

flowers hung around it. Food, water and flowers are offered, but the gifts do not need to be large or expensive – a flower petal or a grain of rice is enough. While they are making puja, Hindus repeat mantras. These are usually verses from the holy books. They begin with the sacred word Aum, which may be used as a mantra on its own. Worshippers do not wear

A Hindu woman making puja at home

shoes, and they stand or sit cross-legged. They may put their hands together and lift them to their chest or forehead, or kneel and touch the ground in front of the murti with their forehead. These are all ways of showing respect.

Other worship

It is part of Hindu belief that God is in everything, so everything which a Hindu does in their life can be counted as worship. This means that even simple everyday tasks like cooking a meal or washing up can be part of worship if they are done properly and with care.

Meditation

Meditation is a way of training and controlling your mind. The aim is to concentrate on God so completely that you stop being aware of

A Hindu boy praying in front of a murti

anything else, even yourself. Meditation is an important part of Hindu worship, and there are instructions in the holy books for ways in which it can be done. In this book, it is explained in more detail on page 24.

New words

Meditation mental control, especially concentrating on God
Murti 'form' – image of a god or goddess which has been specially blessed
Puja worship of a god or goddess
Shrine holy place

Test yourself

What's puja?

What's a murti?

What's meditation?

Things to do

1 What is a shrine? Explain why having a shrine in the house is so important to Hindus.

2 How many ways can you think of in which Hindus show respect to the murti or picture in their shrine?

3 Explain how everyday acts like cooking or washing up can be part of worship for a Hindu.

4 Design a decoration which could be used for a shrine.

Worship II

This section tells you about Hindu worship in temples.

A Hindu temple is called a **mandir**. There are many different sorts of mandir. Some are small and simple, especially in villages where the people are poor. Other mandirs may be very large and beautifully decorated, often with wooden carvings showing scenes from the life of the god. Many temples in India are built where the stories say that a god or goddess lived or appeared to people.

Large mandirs are rather like small villages themselves. There is a main shrine room, and other rooms with shrines to gods who are not so important. Priests need to look after the temple, so there are rooms where they can live. There is always a river or other supply of water, so that people can wash before they go to worship. (This is a special washing to make the people fit for worship. It has nothing to do with being dirty.) Small temples are similar, but they do not have as many rooms. They may have just a shrine room and somewhere for the priest to live.

Worship in the mandir

All Hindu mandirs, even if they are very small, have at least one priest. It is his job to look after the murti, and help the people to worship. Worship often begins before dawn. The murti is 'woken up' and mantras beginning with the sacred word 'Aum' are said. The murti is washed with cold water, dried and has sandalwood paste applied to it. It may have flowers hung on it. If it has been 'asleep' in a separate room, it is moved to the shrine room, and offerings are made to it. Worship may take place several times a day. Hindus believe that even the smallest murti should be worshipped at least once a day.

When worshippers arrive at the temple, they take off their shoes as a sign of respect. They give the gifts they have brought to the priest, who takes them into the shrine room. Ordinary people do not usually go into the shrine room except at festival time. The gifts may be small sums of money, but usually they are things like fruit, nuts or flowers. The worship of some gods and goddesses includes a **sacrifice** of the life of an animal, but this is not usual.

The main tower of a temple in Madurai, India

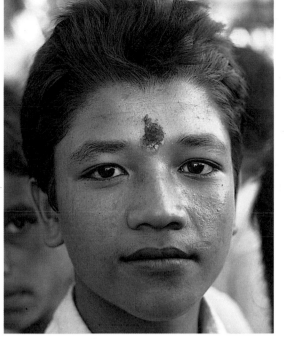

Tilak shows that the person has been to worship

Hindus do not usually worship in groups, but in large temples the priest may sometimes offer prayers in front of a group of people. This worship usually includes three parts which may be put together. The first is **bhajan** which is the singing of hymns, usually from the Vedas. Then there are two forms of worship which use fire. **Havan** means worshipping by making offerings to the god of fire. A fire is lit in a small altar, using small pieces of wood and **ghee** (purified butter). Prayers are said as the fire burns. The other worship is called **arti**. A small tray containing five lights is slowly waved in front of the murti. Then it is taken among to the people who are worshipping. Sometimes they put small gifts of money on the tray. They hold their hands over the flames, then wipe their hands over their head. They believe that by doing this they receive power from the god. Special hymns are sung.

During worship, people place a dot or stripes of special powder on their forehead. This is **tilak** (sometimes called tikka). It shows that the person has been to worship. The shape shows which god they have worshipped. This is not the same as the red dot which many Hindu women place on their forehead, which just shows that they are married.

New words

Arti worship using fire and lights
Bhajan hymn used in worship
Ghee purified butter
Havan worship by making offerings to the god of fire
Mandir Hindu temple
Sacrifice offering to a god or goddess
Tilak mark placed on the forehead during worship

Test yourself

What's a mandir?

What's a sacrifice?

What's tilak?

Things to do

1 Why do you think that gifts to the gods can be things which are small and inexpensive?

2 Write about three ways in which Hindus worship.

3 Imagine you are a Hindu going to a mandir to worship. Write about the things you would see and do.

4 Design a building which would be suitable for use as a mandir.

Pilgrimage

This section tells you about some of the places where Hindus go on **pilgrimage**.

A pilgrimage is a journey which people make for religious reasons. Pilgrimages are often part of Hindu worship and many Hindus feel that going on such a journey is part of their religious duty. There are many different reasons why people choose to go on pilgrimages. They may want to visit a place where the god they worship appeared to people, or where a **miracle** happened. Sometimes they want to pray for something special, and believe that their prayer is more likely to be answered if they are in a holy place.

The Jaganath mandir at Puri

Places for pilgrimage

There are hundreds of places for pilgrimage all over India. Pilgrims may go on a one-day visit to the nearest shrine, or a longer journey to a more important shrine or mandir. Four mandirs in India are often thought to be particularly important. These are thousands of kilometres apart at the four 'corners' of India. Puri on the east coast, Dwarka on the west coast and Badrinath in the north are shrines to Vishnu. Rameshwaram on the south coast is a shrine to Shiva. Many Hindus spend most of their lives saving up to be able to visit all of them. They may be poor and have great difficulties on the journey, but they believe that putting up with the hardships is part of serving God. For the same reason, some Hindus think that for a pilgrimage, it is better to walk. It may be hundreds of kilometres from where they live to the place they want to visit, and may take weeks or even months to walk there, but they believe that the effort makes the pilgrimage more worthwhile. When they arrive at the temple or shrine, many pilgrims crawl round it on their hands and knees. This is to show that they know they have done things in their life which are wrong, and they are sorry. The same sort of worship goes on at all the shrines which the pilgrims visit. They give presents to the god they have come to worship. These are the same sorts of present they would give in worship at home – food, flowers, money.

Holy rivers

Water is necessary for life, and many rivers are respected by Hindus because they believe they are a symbol of God who gives life. Bathing in a holy river is also important, because it washes away **sin** – all the things which a person has done wrong in their life. There are seven holy rivers in India, but the most famous is the River

Ganga (also called the Ganges). Millions of Hindus bathe in its waters, and they believe that drinking even one drop of its water will get rid of all the sins they have committed in this life and in previous lives.

Varanasi

The most important place on the River Ganga is Varanasi, sometimes called Benares. This is where the god Shiva is supposed to have lived, and it is has been a centre for religious teaching for thousands of years. There are special platforms called **ghats** with steps which allow pilgrims to get to the river to bathe or offer puja. Every Hindu hopes to be in Varanasi when they die, and some of the ghats are used for **cremating** dead bodies. After the body has been burned, the ashes will be scattered in the Ganga. The ashes of people who have died elsewhere are often scattered there, too. Hindus believe that this will help the person to break out of the cycle of rebirth.

Worshippers bathing in the River Ganga at Varanasi

New words

Cremate burn a dead body
Ghat steps and platform on a river bank
Miracle event which cannot be explained
Pilgrimage journey for religious reasons
Sin wrong-doing

Test yourself

What's a pilgrimage?

What are ghats?

Which is the most holy river for Hindus?

Things to do

1 What reasons might a Hindu have for wanting to go on a pilgrimage?

2 Explain why Varanasi is so important for Hindus.

3 Why do you think Hindus take home water from the River Ganga to put in their shrine?

4 Find out more about one of the places of pilgrimage mentioned in this section. Your school or local library should have books about India. Write a short article explaining what the place is like, and why it is so important.

Hindu belief

This section tells you something about important Hindu beliefs.

Hinduism is more a way of life than a religion, and its followers do not all believe the same things. The beliefs studied in this unit are ones which almost all Hindus would agree are very important.

Dharma

Hindus believe that life involves a series of duties. These duties are called **dharma**. Dharma is not the same for every person, because it depends on your family background, your job and many other things. It includes things like worshipping God, doing your job properly, not hurting other people or animals, being honest, etc. It is up to every person to do their dharma as well as they possibly can. For Hindus, this is the first aim in life.

Reincarnation

Reincarnation is a very important part of Hindu teaching. It is the belief that when your body dies, your soul (Hindus call it **atman**) moves on to another being. The soul in everything is the same – there is no difference between the soul in a plant or animal and a human being. Hindus believe that the soul moves through a series of 'steps'. It begins in plants and animals, and goes on to human beings. When a man or woman dies their soul is rehoused in another person. This continual cycle of birth and death is called **samsara**.

Karma

The type of person your soul moves on to depends on how you have lived. This is called the law of **karma**. Karma means 'action'. A good karma in your last life will mean a good life this time. A bad karma in your last life will mean a hard life this time. From this comes the belief that there is no point in complaining or being proud of the sort of life you lead. It all comes from the way you behaved in your last life, so is your own responsibility.

Just as this life is decided by your last life, so how you live now will decide what happens next. There is no idea in Hinduism of being judged by God – this is not necessary. How you live will decide whether your next life is a step up or a step down. Steps may be missed out, depending on the karma. Some Hindus believe that doing something very bad will mean your soul is reborn in an animal, and has to work its way up to a human being again. Doing something very good may mean your soul is given a 'rest' before being reborn.

Dharma includes doing your job to the best of your ability

BRAHMAN

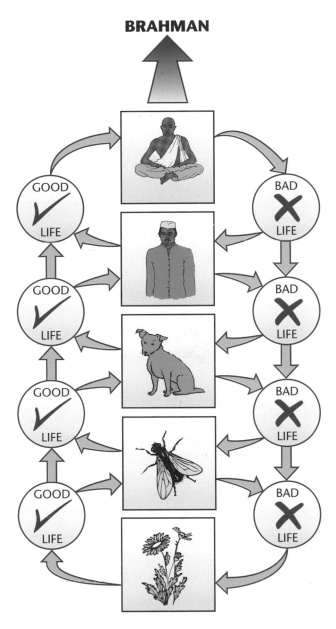

The law of samsara

New words

Atman the soul in everything
Dharma the duties of living
Karma the actions which affect rebirth
Moksha end of the rebirth cycle
Samsara the law of rebirth

Test yourself

What's atman?

What's samsara?

What's moksha?

Things to do

1 What sort of things do you think are your 'duty'? Choose five, and write about them.

2 What is the law of karma? What do you think about the idea that the way you live now affects what will happen to you in your next life?

3 Draw your own diagram to explain the law of samsara.

4 Explain what Hindus believe happens when they reach moksha. Why is this so important?

Moksha

The end of samsara is called **moksha**. It is what every Hindu hopes to achieve. The soul breaks out of the cycle of rebirth, and joins with Brahman. Hindus say that this is like a river merging with the sea. This can only happen when the soul becomes completely pure, and is not affected by anything that happens on earth. Then the soul can go back to being part of Brahman, where it began.

Yogas

This section tells you about the different ways in which Hindus try to achieve moksha.

Moksha is freedom from the cycle of rebirth. Hindus believe that the soul is rehoused in different bodies over and over again until moksha is achieved, and the soul can merge with Brahman. The Bhagavad Gita mentions four paths which lead to moksha. These are the paths of knowledge, meditation, devotion (love of a god or goddess) and action. Each path is open to anyone, and many Hindus use more than one path in their lives – they do not have to choose one and ignore the others.

The path of knowledge – Jnana-yoga

'Knowledge' in this sense means spiritual knowledge rather than just knowing a lot of things. Hindus who follow this path usually need a good teacher. They need to study the religion carefully, and they follow a 'pattern' for their life. This leads them to knowledge of the relationship between the soul (atman) and God (Brahman).

The path of meditation – Raja-yoga

For Hindus, meditation means concentrating so hard that you forget everything around you, and forget even yourself, so that you can reach the real self which is within you. This is the path which has given its name to what most people in Western countries think of as being yoga – the special positions and breathing exercises which clear your mind. The difficulty of this path is that it cannot be followed if you have responsibilities – you cannot concentrate if you are worrying about work or money or family. To ignore your responsibilities goes against Hindu teaching about doing your duty, and means that you would not gain any merit by meditating.

Young Hindus in Britain learning about their religion

Meditation

The path of devotion – Bhakti-yoga

The path of devotion involves choosing a particular god or goddess, and spending your whole life worshipping him or her. This means praying to the god or goddess, offering puja, going on pilgrimages and making sure that all the actions in your life are an offering to him or her.

The path of good works – Karma-yoga

Many Hindus think that for ordinary people, the path of good works is the easiest one to follow. It involves doing your dharma – your 'duty' – to the best of your ability. Dharma is not the same for every person, because it depends on what job you do, what social group you come from and many other things.

The different yogas are all ways in which Hindus may reach Brahman. Hindus do not think that any one path is better than the others, and many follow more than one yoga in their lives. The important thing is to reach Brahman in the end. Many Hindus say that it is like climbing a mountain – which path you choose is not important. Some paths may be steeper or harder to walk up, but different people have different abilities. So long as you reach the top, the achievement is the same – it does not matter how you got there.

Test yourself

How many paths does the Bhagavad Gita mention?

What's Jnana-yoga?

What's Bhakti-yoga?

Things to do

1 Explain what Hindus aim to achieve by meditation.

2 Why do you think many Hindus feel that the path of Karma-yoga is the easiest to follow?

3 Choose one of the yogas mentioned in this section. Try to find out more about it, and write a short article explaining why you think that it helps Hindus to concentrate on Brahman.

4 Any Hindu is able to choose whichever path they wish, to work towards their aim of achieving moksha. How many reasons can you think of why Hinduism is such an open religion?

Hindu life

This section looks at two ways in which religion affects a Hindu's life.

Ashramas

According to Hindu teaching there are four **ashramas** – stages of life. The first stage is the student. From the age of about eight to about twenty, young people should study and learn about the religion. They are then fit to take their place as adults, and go on to the next stage, which is called **grihastha**. This is the householder stage, when a person is expected to earn their living, marry, and have a family. As they get older (some people think at about the

age of 50) they are expected to leave friends and family behind and go and live on their own in a place where they can have peace and quiet. This is the stage called **vanaprastha**. They should give up all kinds of pleasure, because the idea is to begin to prepare to leave the body at death. Anything which gives the body pleasure should therefore be left behind, and the person should begin to concentrate only on their religion. The last stage is that of the holy man or **sannyasin**. A sannyasin has no fixed home, and as few possessions as possible – usually just the clothes he wears and a bowl for his food. He has no responsibilities or family ties, so he is able to concentrate entirely on his religion.

Although this is the 'ideal' life, many Hindus cannot afford to live their lives like this, or do not wish to do so. For all but a few Hindus, the student years end long before the age of twenty. Many Hindus do not wish to give up everything they enjoy in their lives, and so continue in the grihastha stage until they die. Only a few Hindus go on to the third stage, and even fewer become sannyasins.

The idea of the four stages of life is based on the most important Hindu teaching that the aim of everyone's life is moksha – joining with Brahman. This can only be achieved when the person is no longer affected by things in the world – in other words, is ready to give up the world. By the time they reach the stage of the sannyasin, a Hindu has had sufficient experience of the world to be able to judge the best and worst of life. They can therefore decide on the basis of experience whether or not they want to give up the world.

A sannyasin

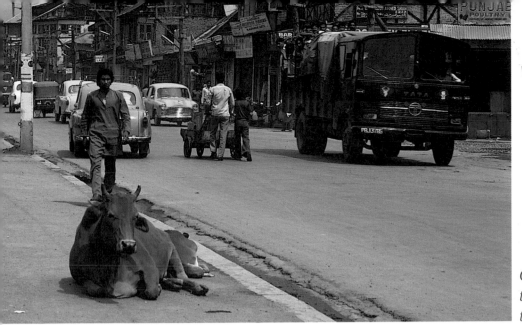

Cows are allowed to wander where they like

Respect for all life

Hindus respect all life, because of their belief in reincarnation. This means that many Hindus – though not all – are vegetarian. They do not eat meat because they believe that it is important to respect the life of animals. Even if they eat other sorts of meat, no Hindu will eat beef. This is because to a Hindu, the cow is sacred. No one really knows the reason for this, but it is probably partly because the white cow is a symbol of atman – the soul which is present in everything. In India, cows are protected because they are sacred. They are milked, and cow dung is used as a fertilizer and is often dried to use as fuel, but cows themselves are never killed for food. They are allowed to wander where they like, even in towns and cities, and there are severe punishments for killing a cow, even in an accident.

New words

Ashrama stage of life (Hindus believe there are four)
Grihastha second stage of life – 'householder'
Sannyasin holy man
Vanaprastha the third stage of life

Test yourself

What are ashramas?

What's a sannyasin?

What's a vegetarian?

Things to do

1 Explain the four stages of life which a Hindu may follow. Why do you think not all Hindus follow all of them?

2 What sort of things do you think it would be hardest to leave behind when a Hindu enters the stage of vanaprastha? Explain why they may take this step.

3 Why are many Hindus vegetarian?

4 How many reasons can you think of why the cow should be so important in India? Use encyclopaedias and books about India to try to find out more.

Festivals I

This section tells you about the festival of Divali.

Hindu calendars are based on the changes in the moon. Most Hindu festivals take place in the middle of the month when the moon is full, or at the very end when it is just about to return as the new moon. India is an enormous country, and it is important to remember that festivals are not celebrated in the same way in different parts of the country. They may also be celebrated differently by Hindus living in other parts of the world. In particular, the same festival may be used by different groups of Hindus to remember different stories. For almost all Hindus, Divali is the most important festival in the year.

Divali

Divali takes place at the end of the month of Ashwin, and carries on into the month of Kartik (October–November in the western calendar). In some places it is a three-day festival, but it usually lasts for five days. It includes the beginning of the financial year.

'Divali' means lights, and throughout the festival Hindus decorate their homes, mandirs and other buildings with rows of lights. In the past, small clay lamps called divas were used, and this gives the festival its name. Today, small electric lights are often used instead.

Like many other Hindu festivals, Divali remembers several different stories. One of the most popular stories is from the Ramayana. It tells how Prince Rama won the battle against his enemies, and found his wife Sita. They returned home and Rama was crowned king. Lamps were lit for Rama's victory procession. There are also stories about how the God Vishnu won a battle with the wicked giant Narakasura, and how he tricked a king named Bali who was trying to take over the world. In different parts of India, people think that some of these stories are more important than others, so the festival is celebrated in different ways in different places.

Lighting candles for Divali

Divali is also a time for remembering Lakshmi, the goddess who brings good fortune. She is supposed to visit houses which are clean and tidy, and some people think that the divas are to light her way. She brings good luck throughout the coming year. For people who own shops and businesses, this is especially important, because they believe that Lakshmi helps their businesses do well. Divali comes at the end of the financial year, so they make sure that their account books are up to date and that all their debts are paid. They can then start the new year well, and hope that with Lakshmi's help, it will be a good one.

Divali is a family festival. People give each other presents, and share meals with friends and relations. Sending cards for Divali is becoming more popular, especially with Hindus who live in Britain. There are firework displays and bonfires, with singing and dancing. The idea is to show that darkness can be driven away by light. This is a symbol which shows that evil can be driven away by good.

Test yourself

What does 'Divali' mean?

What are divas?

When does Divali occur?

Things to do

1 Explain why Hindus use lights at Divali.

2 Why is the goddess Lakshmi remembered at Divali?

3 Design a card to send at Divali.

4 Find out more about one of the stories which Hindus remember at Divali. (Books about Hinduism or festivals will help.) Work in small groups and put together a poster or other display to show what you have found out.

Divali celebrations at a temple in Britain

Festivals II

This section tells you about a festival for Krishna's birthday, and festivals which honour the goddess Durga.

Janmashtami

Janmashtami takes place in Shravan, which usually falls in August in the Western calendar. It celebrates the birthday of the god Krishna. The stories about Krishna say that he was born at midnight, so many Hindus spend all night in the temple. At midnight, there is singing and dancing before everyone shares specially-cooked sweets. In many temples, a non-stop reading of the Bhagavad Gita is organized for the eight days and nights before the festival. It takes about three hours to read the Bhagavad Gita all the way through, so a rota of people is needed, with reserves in case anyone is ill. The reading is timed to finish at midnight on Krishna's birthday.

Navaratri

Navaratri takes place in the month of Ashwin, which is September–October in the Western calendar. Its name means 'nine-nights' which is the length of the festival. Like other Hindu festivals, it is used by different groups of Hindus to remember different stories, but most of the celebrations are to honour the Mother Goddess. She is called by several different names (see page 10). For Navaratri, she is remembered as Durga, a fierce soldier who rides into battle on a lion. Anyone who worships Durga as their special goddess keeps the festival with great care. They often eat only one meal a day for the nine days of the festival. Although she is fierce, Durga is also thought to care for people, and so she is the symbol of mothers. In the story of the Ramayana, Prince Rama prays to Durga for help when his wife Sita has been captured. This means that Navaratri is an important time for families. In

A 'baby Krishna' murti in a cradle – part of a temple celebration for Janmashtami

particular, girls who have been married during the past year try to return home at this time. They are given presents. In northern India, there are open-air plays during the festival acting out parts of the Ramayana story to remind people of it. In other places, people dance round a shrine of Durga, which may be specially built for the festival.

Dassehra

Dassehra and Navaratri are sometimes put together as the same festival. 'Dassehra' means 'tenth day', and it falls on the day after the end of Navaratri. During Navaratri God is worshipped through a murti of Durga. At Dassehra this murti is taken to the nearest river and washed. Hindus believe that as it

disappears under the water is takes all their unhappiness and bad luck with it. This makes Dassehra a very happy festival.

Dassehra also remembers the story in the Ramayana of the battle between Prince Rama and the evil demon Ravana. Rama won the

Ravana (Dassehra celebrations in Delhi)

battle with the help of his brother and Hanuman the monkey king, because Durga was on his side. In many places, bonfires and statues of Ravana are burned. In Delhi, the capital of India, there is an enormous firework display at Dassehra. The main part of the celebrations is the burning of a wooden statue of Ravana 30 metres high.

Like all Hindu festivals, there is a serious lesson behind all the enjoyment. The story of the Ramayana is the story of how good wins over the powers of evil, and reminds people of God's love. During Dassehra Hindus try to make up any quarrels they may have had during the past year.

Test yourself

How long does it take to read the Bhagavad Gita all the way through?

What does Navaratri mean?

What does Dassehra mean?

Things to do

1 Why do you think many Hindus choose to spend the night celebrating Krishna's birth in the temple?

2 Why did Rama pray to Durga when his wife had been captured?

3 Give three reasons why Dassehra is such a happy festival.

4 Explain the lesson which these festivals teach. What do you think about having a special time when people try to make up any quarrels they may have had?

Festivals III

This section tells you about other Hindu celebrations.

Holi

Holi is a spring festival. It is celebrated by Hindus all over the world, although they remember different stories in their celebrations. Many Hindus remember stories about when Krishna was young. He often used to play tricks on people, so Holi is a time for practical jokes. A favourite trick with children is to throw coloured powders and water over people in the streets. There are often water-fights as people join in the fun.

A more serious story gives the festival its name. Holika was a princess who tried to kill Prahlada, a great follower of Vishnu. Prahlada was saved because he chanted the names of God. This story reminds Hindus how important it is to trust God.

Raksha Bandhan

At Raksha Bandhan, a sister ties a coloured silk or cotton bracelet around her brother's wrist.

Raksha Bandhan

She hopes that it will protect him, and it is a sign that he will protect her. The custom recalls the story of the god Indra, who was attacked by an evil demon. He was saved because his wife had tied a magic string around his wrist.

Ramnavami

Ramnavami is the birthday festival of the God Rama. Rama is a very popular god for Hindus, and he is often worshipped at the shrines in people's homes. If they can, Hindus go to the temple for Ramnavami to worship there, too. There are readings from the Ramayana. A special part of the worship is the singing of the Ramanama, which is a list of all the names of Rama.

Like many other Hindu festivals, Ramnavami is a day of **fasting**. For Hindus fasting means going without certain foods. These are foods like meat, fish, onions, garlic, rice, wheat and pulses. Foods which are allowed on fast days are things like fresh fruit, milk and ghee. These are foods which many poor Hindu families could not normally afford, so eating them is a way of making festivals more special.

Special patterns are made at New Year

New Year

Hindus may celebrate New Year at different times, depending whereabouts in India they live or came from. The beginning of the calendar year is different from the beginning of the financial year. Whenever New Year occurs, it is always seen as the chance to turn over a new leaf and make changes in your life. Families get up very early, and often make special puja. Houses are cleaned and often painted, and everyone wears new or clean clothes. Coloured chalks or flours are used to make patterns on the floor, which Hindus hope will bring happiness throughout the year to come.

Hindus celebrate many other festivals. Some are important in a particular area, or to worshippers of a particular god. Most festivals involve making special puja, and many involve fasting.

New word

Fast go without food for religious reasons

Test yourself

Who gave Holi its name?

What does Raksha Bandhan mean?

Whose birthday is remembered at Ramnavami?

Things to do

1 Why is Holi a time for practical jokes? What sort of things often happen?

2 Explain why girls tie a bracelet around their brothers' wrists at Raksha Bandhan.

3 How many reasons can you think of why New Year should be an important festival?

4 Hindus believe that New Year is a time to make changes in your life. Work in pairs to think of five changes it would be a good idea for you to make. Write about what you have chosen, and say why.

Hindu history

This section tells you something about the history of Hinduism.

Hinduism is now the religion of most people who live in India, and the history of the country and the religion are very closely connected.

How Hinduism began

Hinduism did not 'begin' – it developed gradually over many hundreds and even thousands of years. About 4000 years ago, the people who lived in what today is called India worshipped many gods from the world around them. They were gods like fire, water and wind. Then the northern part of the country was taken over by invaders, who brought their religion with them. This involved worship of the sun, moon and sky. Over many years, these two religions gradually joined together. People did not stop worshipping their own gods, but they began worshipping other gods, too. Over hundreds of years, the idea developed that these gods were not really different beings, they were different ways of looking at the same thing. They were all ways of showing Brahman, the Great Power.

Hinduism stayed like this for hundreds of years. Then people became dissatisfied, and began to think that other religions had more to offer,

especially the new system of thought begun by Gotama, the Buddha. Under the **Buddhist** emperor Asoka, in the third century BCE, almost the whole of India was Buddhist. Hinduism had to change. The Vedas and stories like the Ramayana and the Mahabharata were written down, so they became easier to remember and retell. Important teachers spent their lives teaching about these and other stories. People began to learn the lessons behind the stories. Hindu beliefs gradually became clearer, and Hinduism became popular again.

How Hinduism developed

Between the twelfth and sixteenth centuries CE, India was invaded three times. This time the invaders were **Muslims**, followers of the religion of Islam. They ruled India for 300 years after the third invasion. They did not like some of the ways in which Hindus worshipped, and destroyed many Hindu temples. During the time they ruled India, Hinduism became less popular, because many people became Muslims.

The next rulers of India were the British. They began as traders but gradually took over more and more power and became full rulers of the country in 1857. For the next hundred years,

Havan (offerings to the god of fire) is still an important part of Hindu worship

Muslim refugees crowding a train from Delhi to Pakistan in 1947

they controlled India. In that time there were many changes. Hinduism had to change, too, as some of the old ideas were challenged. During the nineteenth century, important teachers like Vivekananda began presenting Hinduism as a world religion. In the twentieth century, the Hindu leader Mahatma Gandhi was one of the most important people to shape the history of the country.

When India became independent in 1947, the country was divided. A new country called Pakistan was created, to be a Muslim country. Many Hindus who were living in that area moved back to India, many Muslims living in India moved to Pakistan. It was a time of great suffering and bitterness, and thousands of people were killed in riots. Since that time, India has been mainly Hindu.

Hinduism is a mixture of many different beliefs and customs. They have come together over thousands of years to make one religion. This is one reason why Hinduism is a very tolerant

religion, and accepts many different views. Hindus say that all religions are a search for truth, and everyone has to find out the truth for themselves.

New words

Buddhist follower of Buddhism
Muslim follower of the religion of Islam

Test yourself

Who was Asoka?

When did India become independent?

Which new country was created?

Things to do

1 Explain how the religion of the people of northern India become combined with the religion of the people who invaded.

2 What things happened in the time of Asoka which meant that Hinduism eventually became stronger?

3 Why do you think that creating the new country of Pakistan caused so many problems?

4 Most Hindus say that the most important part of religion is that you should work out the truth for yourself. Write a short story which shows how you believe something far more if you have found it out for yourself.

The caste system

This section tells you about the different groups of people in India.

Hinduism teaches that different people have different abilities. What these are depends mainly on their previous lives. Hinduism also teaches that it is important for each person to make the most of their abilities. This led to an idea that particular groups of people had particular talents, and for hundreds of years, people in India have been divided into groups. These groups are called **varnas**, and they have been an important part of the way the country of India has been organized. There are four main groups, and at first they were probably quite separate.

The first and most important group were **Brahmins**. They were best at being priests, and jobs which involve giving advice. The second group were **Kshatriyas**, who were soldiers and people who rule the country. The **Vaishyas** were shop-keepers, traders and farmers. The lowest of the four were the **Shudras**, who were servants for the other three groups. Gradually, these groups divided into many smaller groups called **jatis** or **castes**. Your jati depends on your job. Jobs are passed on in families, so a son usually does the same job as his father. Different jatis are 'higher' or 'lower' than others. People in 'higher' jatis are thought to be more pure than those in lower jatis. Today, some people are still very strict about not having anything to do with groups which are less pure than their own. For example, they will not marry someone from a lower jati, and anything they eat must have been prepared by someone from the same jati.

Brahmins

The highest group are Brahmins, and Hindu priests usually come from this group. Today, many Brahmins do other jobs. The fact that they are the highest group means that Brahmins tend to keep the rules about caste more strictly than other Hindus. For example, a Brahmin cannot eat certain foods unless they have been cooked by another Brahmin, and they are not supposed to drink alcohol.

Priests are usually Brahmins

Harijans

The lowest group of all in Hinduism are the **Harijans**. They are below the other four groups, and do the dirtiest jobs. For example, many Harijans work with leather, which no 'higher' Hindu would do. For many years, other Hindus would not have anything to do with Harijans. They were called '**untouchables**'. In the early years of the twentieth century, the Hindu leader Gandhi worked hard to improve the lives of untouchables. He gave them the name 'Harijans', which means 'children of God'.

This way of dividing people into groups is called the **caste system**. It is the way that people in India have lived for hundreds of years. In the past 50 years, things have changed. More people travel away from their home area, and live and work in cities. In factories and shops, they have to meet and talk with people who are not from their own group. The rules cannot be kept so strictly. Now many Brahmins are not priests, not all members of the army are Kshatriyas and many people who are not Vaishyas own shops. Apart from Brahmins and Harijans, many people are not very interested in what varna they are, but they know what jati they belong to, and what this means in their dealings with other people. Since 1947, it has been against the law in India to treat former untouchables differently, but it takes a long time to change the way people think, and changes in the law are not always enough. In many villages in India the caste system is still very strict.

New words

Brahmins priests (first varna)
Caste another name for a jati
Caste system name given to the organization of varnas and jatis
Harijans Gandhi's name for untouchables
Jati part of a varna
Kshatriyas second varna
Shudras fourth varna
Untouchables lowest group of people
Vaishyas third varna
Varna one of four main groups

Test yourself

What is the first varna?

What is the fourth varna?

What does 'Harijan' mean?

Things to do

1 Why do you think that Brahmins tend to keep the rules about caste more strictly than many other groups?

2 How many reasons can you think of why Hindus would not want to work with leather?

3 Why do you think Gandhi called the untouchables 'children of God'?

4 Look for examples in newspapers or on TV of an occasion or a place where people are treated differently because of their background. What do you think about this? Write a letter to an imaginary newspaper giving your views.

Mahatma Gandhi

This section tells you about a famous Hindu.

One of the most important Hindus in the last hundred years was a man called Mohandas Karamchand Gandhi. He was an important leader in India at the time when the country was becoming independent, and he did much to shape the way Hindus thought about themselves.

Gandhi's early life

Mohandas Gandhi was born on 2 October 1869, in a small town in western India. He was the youngest son in the family. Although they were not high in the caste system, his family were

Gandhi with his wife in 1913

important in the local area, and they were quite well off. Gandhi's parents were strict Hindus, and he was brought up to worship Vishnu.

As a boy, Gandhi was very shy and timid. He did not do particularly well at school because of this. In those days, marriages between children were common in India, and when he was thirteen, Gandhi's parents arranged his marriage to a girl called Kasturbai. At first, he and his wife did not get on, and because he was at school they spent more time apart than they were together. As they grew up, however, they became very close.

When Gandhi was sixteen his father died, and the family became short of money. He had to find some way of earning his living, and a friend suggested he should go to England to study law. At first his family was against the idea, but he persuaded them, and Kasturbai sold her jewellery to buy his ticket. After three years in London, he passed his exams, and returned to India in 1891.

Gandhi's work

Back in India, life was difficult, and after two years he was offered a chance to go and work in South Africa. There he began to realize that coloured people were being treated unfairly. This is called **discrimination**. When his law work was finished, he decided to stay in South Africa to try to improve the way Indians were being treated there. He worked there for the next twenty years. He became well-known as a writer, and fighter for freedom. His idea of fighting was not the same as other people's, however. He said that violence was wrong, and instead he talked about **ahimsa** – non-violence and respect for life. He taught that it is important to stand up for what you believe, but this does not mean that you have to fight for it with violence.

Gandhi's body was surrounded by rose petals

By the time Gandhi went back to India in 1915, he was very well known. A famous Indian poet called him 'Great Soul', and for the rest of his life he was known by the Indian word for this – **Mahatma**. He began working to improve life for the millions of people in India who were very poor. He said that it was wrong to call people 'untouchable' and gave them the new name 'Harijan', which means 'children of God'.

Gandhi played an important part in the talks about India becoming independent, and did his best to calm the fighting and riots between Hindus and Muslims when the new country of Pakistan was created. Some Hindus felt so strongly that Pakistan should not have been created that they wanted to fight to try to win it back. They knew that Gandhi would never agree to this. A man called Nathuram Godse decided that the only answer was to get rid of Gandhi. On 30 January 1948, when Gandhi was talking to a huge crowd in Delhi, Godse shot him three times. Gandhi died at once. His funeral took place the next day, and over three million people took part in the funeral procession. Today, Gandhi is remembered and respected as a man of peace not only by Hindus, but by people all over the world.

Test yourself

What's discrimination?

What's ahimsa?

What does Mahatma mean?

Things to do

1 Why did Gandhi decide to stay on in South Africa when his law work was finished?

2 What does the fact that he was called 'Mahatma' tell you about Gandhi?

3 What are the advantages and disadvantages of Gandhi's idea of 'ahimsa' – standing up for what you believe without fighting?

4 Find out more about the life of Gandhi. How did he show the teachings of Hinduism in his work? Work together in groups to do a project, illustrated with pictures.

New words

Ahimsa non-violence
Discrimination treating someone unfairly
Mahatma 'great soul' (title given to Gandhi)

Hindus in Britain

This section tells you something about Hindus in Britain.

There are about 350,000 Hindus in Britain today. Most come from families who have moved to Britain from India in the last 50 years. After World War II, people from many countries were encouraged to come to Britain because British industries were short of workers. Of course, they brought their religions with them.

In India, praying and worshipping as part of a group is not something which happens very often except at some of the major temples. For Hindus living in Britain, meeting other people who share the same religion and background is important, so Hindus have started meeting together for worship. These meetings usually take place on a Sunday, because this fits into the British way of life. There are now about 150 mandirs in Britain. They are expensive to build, so most are in buildings that have been altered so that they can be used as temples. Most mandirs in Britain are dedicated to Krishna or Rama.

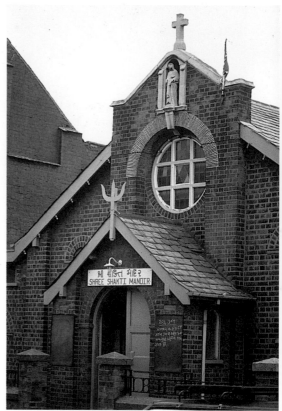

Many Hindu temples in Britain are in buildings that have been altered

Inside a Hindu temple in Preston, UK

Hinduism is based in the home. When most of the people around are not followers of Hinduism, this becomes even more important. Children learn their religion from the way their parents follow it. As in India, every Hindu home in Britain has a shrine. If the family can afford it, this is a separate room. If not, it can be just a shelf on the wall, usually in the kitchen or a bedroom. Family puja takes place there, just as it does in India.

Hindu women

Hindu women are highly respected. Hindus believe that the most important job a woman can do is to run the house and look after the family. Hindu women are encouraged to have a good education, and in Britain many are doctors and teachers.

Hare Krishna

Hindus do not usually persuade other people to join their religion, but Hinduism has gained a lot of interest from people in the West. Many people have joined groups led by **gurus**. A guru is a religious leader, often a man who teaches about a particular part of Hinduism. One of the groups most often seen in Britain is usually called Hare Krishna. This is the name given to followers of the guru called **Swami** Prabhupada. (Swami is a title used for Hindu holy men.) He began the International Society for Krishna Consciousness (ISKCON) in 1967, and all its temples are run by Westerners who have **converted** to Hinduism. Swami Prabhupada explained Hindu teachings about finding your real self by saying that most people live their lives as if they were asleep. When people are asleep, they forget what they are like when they are awake. In the same way, most people do not know what they really are, and need to 'wake up' to find their real self. Swami Prabhupada said that the way to do this was to repeat a mantra of the names of Krishna. This becomes a form of meditation. Followers of Hare Krishna believe that everything they do in their life is an offering to Krishna. They live strictly and simply. There are members of the group in many British cities, easily recognized by their yellow robes.

A Hare Krishna procession in London

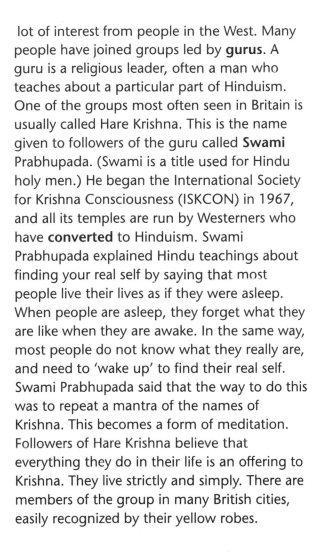

New words

Convert to become a member of a religion
Guru religious teacher
Swami title given to Hindu holy men

Test yourself

What's a guru?

What's a swami?

Who began the Hare Krishna movement?

Things to do

1 Explain why Hindus in Britain often meet together for worship. Why does this normally take place on a Sunday?

2 Why do you think family life is so important for Hindus in Britain?

3 How many reasons can you think of why Hindus might consider it a particularly important job to look after the home and family?

4 Why is it important to followers of Hare Krishna that they should live strict lives?

5 If possible, invite a Hindu who lives in Britain to come and talk to your group about their life and their beliefs. Remember to prepare questions in advance!

Special occasions I

This section tells you about important things which happen to young Hindus.

The special ceremonies which are performed throughout a Hindu's life are called **samskars**. Altogether, there are sixteen samskars which are performed at various times during a person's life. Hindus hope that these ceremonies will improve the person's karma (place in the cycle of rebirth). Like most important Hindu ceremonies, the correct way of performing them is laid down in the Scriptures.

Before birth

Even before a baby is expected, the couple pray about the kind of child they would like. The first three samskars are performed during pregnancy. They are prayers that God will protect the mother and the baby, so that the child will be born healthy.

Birth

When the baby is born, he or she is washed, and then their father places a few drops of honey and ghee in their mouth, using a gold ring. Then he recites a prayer from the Scriptures. In some places, the sacred syllable 'Aum' is written on the baby's tongue with honey, using a special pen. This is the syllable which begins all prayers, so it is like saying that the baby's life will be a prayer. For most Hindus it is important to note the exact time and place of birth, as this will be used by the priest who prepares the baby's **horoscope**. A horoscope is a way of telling the future based on the positions of the stars. Many Hindus use horoscopes in their life to find out the best time for events to take place.

The naming ceremony

The baby is given its name at a special ceremony, usually when it is twelve days old. Choosing the name is very important, because the right name will bring the child luck. A priest is often asked to suggest an initial or syllable which would be suitable. The baby is dressed in new clothes, and placed in a cradle. The ceremony itself is very simple – the name is announced by the eldest woman in the family, and the baby's father says into the baby's ear, 'Now your name is ... .' Songs are sung, and a special sweet made of fruit, nuts and sugar is given to friends and relatives who have come to the ceremony.

The next three samskars take place as the child grows. The ninth samskar takes place with the baby's first hair-cut, which is usually when it is about a year old. For a boy, this means having his whole head shaved. It is a symbol of removing any bad karma from his previous life.

Shaving a boy's head is the ninth samskar

A father giving the sacred thread to his son

The thread ceremony

This is the tenth samskar, and is a very important ceremony for boys in the three higher varnas. Members of the lower castes do not take part in this ceremony. In India it usually takes place sometime between a boy's seventh and twelfth birthday, but the exact age may vary. The sacred thread – a loop of cotton – is hung over the left shoulder, so that it hangs down to the right hip. Once he has been given this thread, a boy is counted as a man. He can read the Vedas and carry out religious ceremonies. He wears the thread for the rest of his life, changing it at festivals.

A·guru prepares the boy for this ceremony, and prays for the boy before he is given the thread. Then he becomes the boy's teacher whilst he studies the Scriptures. Some boys spend several years studying. The thread ceremony is the time when a boy joins the religion, so it is the reason why members of the three highest varnas are sometimes called 'twice-born'. They have had a spiritual (religious) birth as well as a physical one.

New words

Horoscope way of telling the future based on the stars
Samskars ceremonies of life

Test yourself

How many samskars are there?

What's a horoscope?

What is the sacred thread?

Things to do

1 Hindu children are often given the names of gods and goddesses. Why do you think this is so?

2 Explain what happens at the thread ceremony. Why is this so important?

3 Explain why members of the three higher varnas are called 'twice-born'.

4 Many people read horoscopes in newspapers and magazines. Working in small groups, discuss the reasons why people do this. Do you think 'star signs' have any real meaning?

Special occasions II

This section tells you about Hindu teachings on marriage.

Hindus think it is important to marry, so that there can be children who can carry on the family. Parents usually choose who their children will marry. They are thought to know best, because they have had more experience of life. This is called an **arranged marriage**. The parents often take the advice of a priest, and may use the couple's horoscopes to make sure that they are well matched. In the past, couples did not meet until their wedding day. Today, things are not as strict as they once were, and the couple may suggest a possible partner, or have met a few times.

The first step of a Hindu marriage is the ceremony to announce the engagement. The men from both families meet. There are readings from the Vedas, and prayers are said. The ceremony ends with a meal.

A Hindu bride wears beautiful jewellery

The wedding

The wedding ceremony usually lasts about an hour, but the celebrations often go on for several days. The wedding takes place either in a temple or the bride's home. The bride wears special eye make-up, and a dye is used to make patterns on her hands and feet. She wears a new red and gold **sari**, and lots of gold jewellery. Preparing the bride for the ceremony takes several hours. Both the bride and groom wear garlands of flowers.

The first part of the wedding is when the bride's father welcomes the bridegroom. The bridegroom sits under a special canopy, which is a decorated covering. He is given small presents which are symbols of happiness and a good life. Then the bride arrives, usually wearing a veil so her face cannot be seen. She removes this during the ceremony. The couple sit in front of a

special fire. Their right hands are tied together and holy water is sprinkled on them when the bride's father 'gives' her to the bridegroom. There are prayers and offerings of rice.

The most important part of the ceremony is when the bride and groom take seven steps

The couple's right hands are tied together

The bride and groom sit under a special canopy

towards the fire. At each step they stop and make promises to each other. While they do this, they are joined by a piece of cloth. It is hung loosely round the bridegroom's neck, and tied to the bride's sari. This is a symbol that they are being joined as husband and wife. Once they have taken the steps together, they are married. There are more prayers and readings, and flower petals are thrown before the guests give their wedding presents. Then everyone shares a meal. After she is married, the bride is counted as belonging to her husband's family.

Divorce

Indian law allows divorce, but strict Hindus do not accept any ending of a marriage except death. It is seen as a disgrace to both families if the couple divorce.

New words

Arranged marriage marriage where the partners are chosen or suggested by relatives
Sari long piece of cloth worn as a dress

Test yourself

How long does a Hindu wedding take?

What's a sari?

Where do the bride and groom sit?

Things to do

1 What is an arranged marriage? Think of three disadvantages and three advantages of an arranged marriage.

2 Explain why the couple are joined by the scarf whilst they make their promises.

3 What happens in the most important part of the wedding ceremony?

4 Design a wedding card which would be suitable to send to a Hindu couple.

5 If possible, talk to a Hindu couple about their wedding. They may have photos which you could look at.

45

Special occasions III

This section tells you about what happens when a Hindu dies.

Hindus believe in rebirth, so they think that the body is not needed after death. Death is seen as being a welcome release from life, so a funeral is a time for looking forward, as well as a time of sadness because the person is no longer with people who love them. India is a hot country, so it is the custom for Hindu funerals to be on the day after death, before the body decays.

Hindu funerals

When someone dies, their body is washed and wrapped in a cloth called a **shroud**. A garland of flowers is often placed on the body, and it is put on a special stretcher. Then it is taken to be cremated. It is placed on a special fire called a **funeral pyre**. If possible, the funeral pyre is built on a ghat by one of the sacred rivers. A ghat is a special platform at the bottom of steps leading to the river. If there is no running water, there is a cremation ground outside every town or village.

The eldest son walks round the funeral pyre three times carrying a lighted torch, then he sets the pyre alight. Ghee is used to help the flames burn. Families who can afford it include blocks of sandalwood in the pyre, which burn with a sweet smell. The people say prayers, and there are readings from the Scriptures reminding the mourners that everyone who dies will be reborn. The closest male relative stays at the pyre until the fire has gone out, then he collects the ashes. All Hindus hope that they will be in Varanasi when they die, and that their ashes will be scattered on the River Ganga. They believe that this will save them many future rebirths.

In many Indian cities, and for Hindus living in the West, bodies are not burned in the open air, but are taken to a **crematorium**. Important customs like walking around the body with a lighted torch are carried out at the undertakers. The ashes are collected after the body has been cremated. Many Hindus living in other countries have the ashes of their relatives flown back to India so that they can be scattered on the Ganga.

A Hindu funeral arriving at a cremation ground

Funeral ghats on the banks of the River Ganga at Varanasi

The kriya ceremony

After the funeral, the relatives of the person who has died return home and bathe. Death is thought to make anyone who has been near the body unclean, so the relatives do not go out and meet people until all the ceremonies are over. The last ceremony takes place ten or twelve days after the funeral. It is called the **kriya ceremony**. Rice and milk are made into offerings, not just for the person who has died, but for everyone in the family who has died in the past. Rice is an important food, and milk comes from the sacred cow. Once this ceremony has been held, the person's soul is believed to have been rehoused in another body, so the family can return to normal.

New words

Crematorium place where dead bodies are burned

Funeral pyre pile of wood for burning a body

Kriya ceremony final ceremony after a death

Shroud piece of cloth wrapped around a dead body

Test yourself

What's a shroud?

What's a crematorium?

When is the kriya ceremony held?

Things to do

1 Explain why Hindus see death as being a time of hope as well as a time of sadness.

2 Why do relatives try to make sure that ashes are scattered on the River Ganga?

3 What is the kriya ceremony? Why is it so important?

4 How many reasons can you think of why the offerings at the kriya ceremony are of rice and milk?

5 Find out more about the city of Varanasi. (Books about India and Hinduism will help.) Why is it so important to Hindus?

Glossary

Ahimsa non-violence
Arranged marriage marriage where the partners are chosen or suggested by relatives
Arti worship using fire and lights
Ashrama stage of life (Hindus believe there are four)
Atman the soul in everything
Aum sacred Hindu word

Bhajan hymn used in worship
Brahman the Great Power
Brahmins priests (first varna)
Buddhist follower of Buddhism

Caste another name for a jati
Caste system name given to the organization of varnas and jatis
Convert to become a member of a religion
Creator one who makes things
Cremate burn a dead body
Crematorium place where dead bodies are burned

Dharma the duties of living
Discrimination treating someone unfairly

Eternal lasting for ever

Fast go without food for religious reasons
Funeral pyre pile of wood for burning a body

Ghat steps and platform on a river bank
Ghee purified butter
Grihastha second stage of life – 'householder'
Guru religious teacher

Harijans Gandhi's name for untouchables
Havan worship by making offerings to the god of fire
Horoscope way of telling the future based on the stars

Jati part of a varna

Karma the actions which affect rebirth
Kriya ceremony final ceremony after a death
Kshatriyas second varna

Mahatma 'great soul' (title given to Gandhi)
Mandir Hindu temple
Mantra short sacred text or prayer
Meditation mental control, especially concentrating on God
Miracle event which cannot be explained
Moksha end of the rebirth cycle
Murti 'form' – image of a god or goddess which has been specially blessed
Muslim follower of the religion of Islam

Pilgrimage journey for religious reasons
Preserver one who keeps things from decay
Puja worship of a god or goddess

Reincarnation belief that a soul is reborn
Rig Veda first and most important of the Vedas

Sacred very holy
Sacrifice offering to a god or goddess
Samsara the law of rebirth
Samskars ceremonies of life
Sannyasin holy man
Sanatan dharma 'eternal truth'
Sanskrit old language
Sari long piece of cloth worn as a dress
Shrine holy place
Shroud piece of cloth wrapped around a dead body
Shudras fourth varna
Sin wrong-doing
Soul a person's spirit
Swami title given to Hindu holy men
Symbol something which stands for something else

Tilak mark placed on the forehead during worship
Trimurti 'the three gods' – Brahma, Vishnu and Shiva

Untouchables lowest group of people

Vaishyas third varna
Vanaprastha the third stage of life
Varna one of four main groups
Vedas Hindu holy books